Black Man Abroad: The Toulouse Poems

BLACK MAN ABROAD:

THE TOULOUSE POEMS

By

James A. Emanuel

LOTUS PRESS
Detroit
1978

Cover photographs by Maurice Lévy

LOTUS PRESS

Post Office Box 601
College Park Station
Detroit, Michigan 48221

"Flower of a New Nile"

For Marie-France

PREFACE

I am strongly aware of the transitional nature of this book. *The Treehouse and Other Poems* (1968) expressed not only my debt to traditional forms, but also my identification with modern Black consciousness. *Panther Man* (1970) recorded my midstream responses to American racism's nightmarish effect on me as the Sixties ended.

This present volume, with its personal and literary foreshadowings still beyond my grasp, develops some of my unusual 1970-1977 experiences: a stagnating year of uncreativity, two years of revival and reorientation in a foreign land, dramatic shiftings in my renewed American ambience, followed by a revolutionary year of teaching behind the Iron Curtain. The resulting book might be hard to classify as either Black or American in its focus. Yet it contains my longest Black-experience poem: "After the Poetry Reading, Black," written in Poland about a provocative incident in France. My feeling for America is disclosed only in a line of another long poem, " 'The Warsaw Experiment, '75-76': an Unborn Play," which treats the stunning debilitation inherent in totalitarian societies. Other poems were inspired in Ireland, Scotland, England, Spain, and Austria (although three recall Harlem, Manhattan, and Denver). But the hub of the wheel of influence was Toulouse, where I restored my life and my will to write. There a few university colleagues—Anthony Suter, Marvin Holdt, and Lee Audhuy—gave me helpful comments on the poems.

The frequently personal nature of this book squares also with my poetics: a poet should write only what comes feelingly—even if obliquely—out of his own life. A French child moved me to resume poetry writing with "For Alix, Who Is Three"—a reality and memory just as intimate as my involvement with the unyielding theme of my latest poem, "Even Steven...": that adult love, when avoiding forgiveness, has the seeds of both hatred and compassion.

New realities and new concerns are beginning to affect my poetry; but the cruel racism reflected in the Black-oriented poems in this volume has so unforgettably directed my life at crucial points that I can never abandon the challenge to defy and illuminate it. Equally, however, I claim as my very own all the themes that the last several years have forced into *Black Man Abroad: The Toulouse Poems.*

Toulouse, France   *J.A.E.*
1 February 1978

CONTENTS

OCCASIONALS.

THE TOULOUSE POEMS

Part I

It Was Me Did These Things

ride ride ride
and never look back
and don't you ever
don't you ever
stop.

IT WAS ME DID THESE THINGS

Saw this piece of cheese falling
coming hard down on me
from the roof terrace wall
it was weird the way that cheese smelled and sang
and aimed itself right at my staring eye
oh but I was cool that day
stepped aside calm and sure
and saw it heard it smelled it plop right down
and smash smash the sidewalk
then another day I saw this car zooming silly like
taking itself off the street and getting next to me
fast like I was the real enemy
I didn't even think I just stooped down
and it zoomed right up the drugstore window
and went crash crash near some people with their mouths
open
it was a colder day I saw my love
my true true love
kissing another man who wasn't even
holding her close
and I didn't even think
couldn't think it could be that way
nd I didn't cry ever
and if you can believe all that
get on get on your horse
Most Beautiful Horse
ride ride ride
and never look back
and don't you ever
don't you ever
stop.

FOR ALIX, WHO IS THREE

Foreign country of her eyes
picture-book blue
as lakes she fingered while she read
and taught me simple words
like *clé* (like *key*),
chocolate milk breath
curled up in smiles
for such a stranger in the room
who animal by animal
and thing by thing
named big on the page
had to be told again
like *clé* (like *key*),
her voice half gone to bed . . .
    came back transformed in faces that I knew
    or all one changing face in changing years
    one or few or many
    as pages turned and doors swung wide
    row on row on row . . .

And there again was Alix,
who was three
who in foreign country,
of her eyes and chocolate smile
gave me the key
the *clé*
I will throw away
if ever I want
to lock my doors again.

WISHES, FOR ALIX

Always searching,
may you find;
if you run-down,
may you wind;
every year
may you grow
reaping only
what you sow
sowing only in the seed
what will ripen into need
what will sweeten to the touch
seeming little, being much.

May your playmates be a song,
may your friends just skip along
laughing you into their game
letting you remain the same
in their hearts and on their lips
even when their fingertips
have to let you go your way—
glad they saw Alix today.

FRENCH CHILD, BUYING BREAD

(For Anne and Gerard)

Once before, she had taken her mother's place,
lips moving over orders carefully pronounced,
had climbed with lurch and gasp
the single step that brought to fragrant view
the *boulangerie* inside, its sleeping golden rows
and leaning tiers that could be sliced
to feed at once the world she knew;
and holding up her silver franc,
repeating faithfully the words her mother's hand
had patted on her brow,
she had been thrilled not only by the loaf
a different smile had pressed into her arms,
but also by the unexpected flood of gold
returned in tiny coins
the voice of love at home had not foreseen
and must clap hands to see...

This time, to please her mother more,
improving on instructions skipping through her mind,
she took unwavering the step
and from her very own supply of coins
(her mother's franc kept cunningly aside)
held up a golden handful, knowing well
she must receive both bread and coins so plenteous
an extra pocket must be readied for the hoard.

And so her tears could hardly stay
when "Voila!" was a voice
that kindly came down with the bread
but quickly snatched up all but three of her golden coins,
returning nothing—
and later beams of lovelook in her home
could not shine through the mist
in which her mother took her last three coins
("to make it come out right," she said)
and gave her smilingly to keep
one silver franc.

FRANKUDRACKENSTEIN

Her childmouth open,
her stammerscream flew small
against the sudden eye of Monsterman,
dark croucher in her room slow rising forward
till his coldstone shoulder jerked
to almost fit into the sky
that closed across her window.

Pieces of the wall seemed loose
behind his tallow fingers,
ceiling corners crumbling toward his iron hair,
his face a knuckle-hidden post
to batter back the toys
her tightened arms might throw.

Then when her throat
was almost in his fist,
when animals of sound
began to gutter on his lip,
her final strength fell gasp and whirl
enough for leaping
tugging on his hand
and gurgleshouting:

"Do it again, Uncle Romy!
Play the monster!"

DIDN'T FALL IN LOVE

Didn't fall in love,
got out of THAT trap,
took my feet, my socks and boots
OUT,
moved off FAST, whistling toe-tunes
AWAY.

Remembering is tricky:
took our meal sometimes on balcony adrift
on curves of moon, took candlelight
from easy view of towered Saint Sernin
illuminated high and in our night of wine
in sway with music up the leg of couch
that turned our vagrant fingers
to softer play.

Yeah, didn't let those arms
bring me down TOO low,
didn't let that skin touch me
where I REALLY live
when my heartbeat rang
a bell-and-button warning
near your flowing hand.

Didn't look into those eyes
too long, too near, pulled BACK
and traded gulpglance with the wall
with jigsaw-puzzle pictures
Love-And-Kisses never signed;
slid off the couch, glass in my hand,
and never spilled a DROP
and never thought a word about the hand
the fingers free that didn't dare that didn't think.

I started thinking, yeah,
got out of THAT swing,
left treetop stars ablaze,
left our shoes dangling in the air,
let vines we held and crosspiece where we sat
and aimed our toes straight at the moon
hang loose while I took RAINPIPE to the ground,
got DOWN
got OUT of that swing.

Didn't sink into that well
where drink is DROWN,
didn't listen to music
I couldn't dance down,
didn't touch a THING that touches back,
didn't spill a drop of me.

Got back safely to my room
and turned the key on you,
took stone for chair
and sat among the rocks my days remember,
bootless, sockless,
backleaning breathing hard against the risk
of knowing you.

LOVELOOK BACK

Bubble in you
swells beneath my touch,
like air I rode when but a boy
flying on my horse of painted wooden sticks
gulping wind and jumping continents
aiming bit and bridle at the tops of trees.

Look of you tucked in around your eyes
is mystery of books high on the shelf
my tallest ladder never reached,
is words I wondered wide-eyed in the night
when bedroom forms seemed more than chairs
hung down with blue jeans,
rug curled up by shoes.

Sounds that lap me in curtains of your breathing
bring ocean-distance that my prairie years,
in stretching long ago, found borderland
where thirst and drink were same,
where bloodbeat rhythm urged the way
to walk a corner, linger near a skirt,
speak a graceful hunger.

You are cliff and precipice
to hug my narrow path that swayed
through windy stems and darkened in the sun,
that turned from cave I stored with candy
licked until imagination had undressed the town;
you are meadow too for sinking falls
and softest echo in the feel of grass.

Rise of you in slow leave-taking of the room
in gleam of breast and shoulder through tiptoe dark
is body-cover for buds of secret talk
I used to bloom in spaces of my mind
where silent girls slow swung their legs
and played their eyes across my brow.

Leave-taking now is tender part of you
I dare not
touch
but with this hand that once waved
to the hills.

A BIRTHDAY ROSE FOR "MEES"

This rose that sheds some mist for you
does nothing more than I must do.
This rose that stands you in its sun
does little more than I have done,
does nothing more than start the race
that I have run in this still place.
It cannot drop one petal more
than those I've added to my store
of memories affection knows
more intimately than any rose.

FOR "MEES"

Saw your dark hair rise in masses
quicktiming, tapping out your stride
that made that country road a floor to dance on,
dark eyes gulping bites
others nibbled on as scenery . . .
heard your laughing lips draw laughter
at the sparkling tables where your darting words
were wake-up, shake-up music at the champagne lull . . .
felt your hand upon my knee
electrify fatigue as my Volkswagen
climbed and dipped among mysterious hills
and circled down through rain close to the bluest sea . . .
stone stepped you up on the Barcelona blacksmith's dizzy spires,
shared your telescopic eye along the Tarn's deep deepest gorge,
your night-strolling warming touch through its most silent town,
and in the mazy clacky London Underground
made private two-way codes from silly billboard signs.

Then heather on the browning hills
that rose and turned across the riding sky
was brush and mellowrub
with morning light that stroked our windshield
till our hands unjoined
in knowing silent roads of narrow miles
were ours alone (untakeable
by all the Isle of Skye could say
in voice of mountainrock and mist),
would keep for us a corridor of dawn,
a passage back.

Saw you pose among a thousand perfect stones
where legendary giants fought upon the Causeway
in battleboom we drove against in Belfast
(then shaking soldiers from her sleeves,
rolling from her barricaded skirts those drums of steel
and suckling daily, in her years of death, some killer-child)—
all agonies dissolved in Mulligan's Bar
in gin and Joyce and a Dublin cat
who yawned upon the history of his chair.

Cannot cannot forget your memorial ways:
you, disappearing over hills
raised by our quietness
in sentinel moments large and breathless;
you, hip turning slow in Mediterranean sand,
beaching me with glance more whelming than the piling waves;
you, all gentle hand on my doubting shoulder
rebuilding me luminous and possible;
you, in all embraces
kindness ever took from passion,
passion took from dumb despair;
you, the pit and shaft and gleam of sun
in some deep mine of me.

Saw you once in twilight trapped,
a shadowed statue
in your chair of pain,
but still your sadness arch in laughter
lightens, smooth in brilliant phrase;
uncatchable in neatest package of my tightest word,
you burst to what you are,
champagne cork at a table in the sun,
fragrantly gone on sudden crosswind,
the shock of your actual day
falling behind you like a drifting bee.

Can see you now,
long-pencilling some map
your mass of hair is brushing to the bed
you lie upon, tracing highways,
our passage back, where we might
disappear.

FOR MADAME PLASSARD. A THANKS

Looked round my room for something high
to leap from,
to flare me loose from logic of my eyes,
from feel of touchables and harness;
wanted eagle-air to float some words to you.

Uptwisted in my bed, snapped on the light,
put all my spine and tendons
into act of seeing;
saw fruit and flower in wall and drape renew themselves
in bedspread gliding off my feet,
saw leafy candlesticks that toiled to raise their empty pods,
saw shell that rocked and twirled as rainbow tray
or, awaiting ashes, sat and kept its sea-self tame.

Unpeopled all these things; so I reclined
and crossed a bridge to you,
imagining the noise the night the guestroom
changed its shape for me, absorbed the hundred scars
where bed legs, hard moved by unaccustomed hands,
zigzagged their rough geometry.

A bed of rest and quiet, simple thing
and high enough for me to reach and pull aside
far-other drapes that catch all light and shade:
for when I pushed the actual shutters out into the dawn
the words that might have floated in the night
grew plain on barrelled plants, red tile stuck in the grass,
a vine-sucked wall of stone and scores of outlived wooden things
that, leaning, huddled one another.
awaiting shaping hands to make them new.

Among these things that wait for touch,
that stay near grass,
my simple word moves through the dawn
across a bridge to you,
Madame.
You know it well.

LA DAME, AT THE THROW-AWAY FIRE

Nothing that old country shed puked up
was junk to her, was rust, was rag.
While *Madame* slowly lit and smoked a new *Gauloise*
we pried each member loose like stubborn rib
from heavy skeleton that seemed to drag its warrior bones
through wheezing air from mound to mound
defending even dust
our barbarous gloves shook down
and crying exhortations meant for shattered legs,
for marble faces cracked with strain,
waving hoary strength into the stones
that muscled up against our grasp.

We were three against and with *Madame,*
who wore no gloves,
who made the fire herself
but fed it trifles, little flakethings
she poked and pondered with the stick
that rose to tell us what to tug and pull
among her breathing treasures we would junk entire.

La dame made us do heavy battle with an ancient toilet tank
until we wrestled it outside and to the grass
where she lowslapped it with her stick
and bade it live;
likewise no fire, we learned, must touch
the wooden pot Grandfather used beneath the seat
his military poise made tall distinguished chair.

Among us three *La dame's* own daughter,
who was, like him and me, so cruel
to laugh at bedpost angelface and her own babytub alike
while he and I rammed knuckleknees and shoulders
into the silver beards and epaulets
of gentlemen whose mound of portraits
made us curse and sweat to lift
and dodge the slivered glass,
the blackened mouse that
skittered off the cheeks of a midmost sire.

The hoard we would have burned
Madame meant carry up the redbloom path to a different room,
dwindlings resurrecting hands could not make whole:
withered harness in twisting maze, carriage-carcass sunk
and ridden by an earless dwarf of stone
felled across a crushed-in box
neatmarked *biscottes/ouvrir ici;*
her royal stick reprieved
two walnut torsos named for kings
but girdled at the paunch by telephone wires;
it nodded strong to billiard-table legs
wide gargoyle-faced, their sheaths of bitter iron
sardonic browed and lipped in 1810.

When *La dame* spoke we stopped . . .
With her unknowingly
we formed a silent ring
around the laggard fire, the resting stick;
then realworld sunset glow
transformed its common mound of ash
into historic hill we thought to burn,
not knowing what *Madame* had lived to learn:

    We throw away the best we get
    but bury what we save,
    while flames in us give jewel-life
    to all we know of grave.

CLOTHESLINE, RUE MARIE

Skinthings that touch me
with realrub, smells of my moods,
swing arms and legs against the sun,
chest and back spread to the morning air,
wrists and toes uncramped, buttoned at neck
to front the day with upright best of me.

Again my breakfast eyes change tabletop for window,
waver through to plastic yellow ears
two clothespins fix on blue beach towel,
stop shadeful on a purple fig aburst in Neighbor's tree,
come back and sight again from coffee steam
through blur of giant fly spacewalking on the pane
through pocketfold of grey still centering the white
one handkerchief slow dangles from the line;

could stop this time, like times before,
on Neighbor's swelling pears, raspberries
lush against the curvy fence,
grapes about to fall,
springing rows of green that crisp the ground—
or could take steam and blur for sight entire
and mistymake for whole of me
a clothesline-man . . .

Sometimes my arms and legs float calmly
on a line of hours, a playtime lovetime in a lull
that wind forgets while whipping elsewhere to the core;
and when sometimes my limbs are sunk
to lean and wrinkled tossings
airless of joy but hard-dried by the worldly sun,
they yet are crank and tendon of my will to be.

Sometimes in torso I am shirt with wrists pinned down,
twisted by storm on pole that holds the line,
rainwrithing, clinging to changes in the wind,
thin as stripes bared back and front by lightning,
dripdrained to veinlines, to puffbeats gone dry.

Sometimes the buttons at my neck are tight as death
and I would loose them far as toes,
would unwidth, unlength, ungirth all the bounds of me,
let flap and dawdle or do itself to fullness
to a tune from nowhere but my flesh and bone
whatever thing I free and open choose
to give my name as box I sit on, bag I own,
sweat I pour down days that hang
like clothes across the dawn,
waiting
in their purest light
for their clothesline-man,
the best of me.

MY ANIMAL: ACCIDENT AT PAS DE LA CASE

Buttoned animal of me
tossed by ski lift
high on the edge of mountain snow
pawed at my quickening skin,
tumbled my heart,
tugged my body rashly
steeply down the heaving slope
against the edgewise pulling of my mind
till snarling family of skis and legs
stuck ruins into the snow.

My animal,
his hackles straight, shook loose my flesh,
burst upright shedding bones of me
hard grown like bars around his cage
stunned and propped on boots and gloves
while all my sucksoup years
that long had sopped his fangs and melted his claws
sank vapory on my every gasp
as *How to Ski* throbbed into one paragraph on how-to-rise
to rise from huddled humbled pieces
to man erect upon his fears.

Fang and claw
seemed watching me, seemed frosty coils of ire
deepdug into my fragments,
taking hold,
my animal,
in snap and glare of eyes
that warned he smelled the blood
where I felt only pain.
His prison trembled
as my muscles by themselves stretched
for dangling skis,
and strap by strap locked on my wounds,
and knot by knot close tied my animal to me.

From his cage I would not set him free.
Made sure of him while sliding down my pain,
past growling snowclouds,
by rashly yelping at the setting sun
and with my newgrip ski-tip fangs
awkwardly nipping the snowmounds at the end.

CHANTEUSE DE RESTAURANT. TOULOUSE

She sang for us eleven,
long throat of her guitar
slow-pulsing in the door
she filled with lean and tinsel gestures,
a float of rising hair and wing of elbow, hips
that rested on some hidden thing that rocked
as if to soothe her body's moan.

For us alone she moved her face
into the sadness of her song,
then let her eyes from far away
drop down a smile on strings
so sudden jumping stung by joys
guitar was feeling in the night,
strumming her long thigh,
low-stroking tenderly the ears
of us for whom alone she sang
for us, who sopped at nibble-gossip,
swallowed it on spoons,
sucked music from pink glasses,
absently raked crumbs toward the center of our bones
and left our napkins clean of all that lips can do.

Her body changed to clothes we could not chew
and rhythms in her face broke on some foreign shore
our kitchen-vapored hands could never touch,
and music on her brow, far darkening away,
left us entire for lover's arms
that once were all the light she knew,
that strummed her simple skirt
on more guitar than she could hold
and wrapped her last in sadder song.

Then she sang it not to us,
her smile like wafer thin and sweet
for our folded hunger's lick and sprawl,
sang it dimly wondering
if our older bones
had ever once lain in her grass
lovely soaking music from those blades
that greened for her in single sun
and greyed so quickly into song.

On double throbs of her guitar
her downward nods had seen
the final beatings of our hands—
sweet singer drifting seated in the door
as if she had not left us
long ago.

THE TRICK'S AT SEVEN

Hey, Girl!
see me lunching here alone
wringing you out
of my mind, rubbing you off
like butter knifed away?
Noon wine in my head
floats me long back
to loveland impossible we peopled with ourselves,
gave stars unpocketed
by hands we called our own
yet knew as lovers timeless in books,
known even by sunless losers,
even by them who never cared.

Hey, Girl!
see me counting ways to let you go?
adding whats and whys and times ago
we knew it couldn't happen
not to us, to us
and did you ever throw away fresh bread
not thinking,
thinking of the little space between our lives
we sat in softly, folded in,
and closed the eye that watched us unblinking
from some rusty tree that gave hard names
to leaves that wearing green downfell—
that tender space that tumbled us
together, rolled us like happy dice
that turned up seven.

Hey, Girl!
don't you know the trick's at seven?
to guess when game is up,
when mumblekiss advice to shoot again, to pocket crumblings,
to whistlewalk away on easy toes
is teethtalk from the painted Jaw
that chews up what it picks to hear
its withering tale.

Hey, Girl!
see me unravelling you?
picking you off my coat, shaking you out,
making you disappear
and did you ever suck the empty air
that fills the bottom of your glass
not thinking,
thinking How can I ever
can I ever?

Oh, the trick's
at seven!
when flesh alone of us
is thrown and tied
and we are free
to move the pain from bone to bone
and did you ever turn your food away
and feel it right here
burn and swell where
you somewhere still
are touching me.

FLOWERS FOR A REAL-GONE GIRL

Came in the shop sidewise
standing the clerk up
with "I want some flowers"
his nod took in as "Naturally," but changed
right on his neck
when "—flowers that don't live long"
juggled his spine as strange
and gave him no time to dress his face
for "—flowers for my love, true love."

Two pauses, his and mine, took up the slack
that Truth in ordinary clothes allows for growth
and made it fit erect and tight at waist
the moment ticking loud like ancient clock
suddenly all center of the store;
"—flowers red as blood without a name,"
I said, re-licensed him with "for my true true love"
then tethered him to cash-and-carry tree,
leaf and bark of all his link with me,
with "Wrap them tenderly and rich—
in rock as black and hot as summer street
that makes your door a thing to thump and pass
en route to hills."

Fed him his logic and filled his veins
with "Cost is trifling,"
sidestepped his busy lore with "more to the point
is every rock is split at core at last
with softest fingerings,
with silent slow beginnings of the fall,
and in this gentlest lap, this saddest smile of stone,
rest you my heart of flowers,
not wrapped in cellophane, but deeply thrust,
for taking to my love,
into some roughridged trucker's hand
that under garlic breath and bearded smile
will punch the bell and signal that most lovely face
'I'm just the messenger, Lady.
These is for you.' "

GOODBYE NO. 1

As over tea and cakes,
sugarless, lukewarm,
shall we prop ourselves like lean-to,
huddlepool the tag-ends of our love
and friendly sip the lees, sop the crumbs,
brush away the spillings, darts
lipnapkins cannot hold?

Or shall we unsheathe fitful swords of memories:
glitters lean and sizzling,
lightning-slivers in our hearts,
quickwords that once so dug and scarred
while sullen fingers knuckled out of sight
and arms enfolded wooden selves
and legs took steel into their thighs
to back away and stand like fence thrust sudden up?

Not meaning to, these moments try
to keepsake-bind with string
the water where we stand,
roll it giftwrapped,
lightly prettyknotted, laid-away
in curls of tide from days we were the gold
and loved ourselves as treasure
for each other.
Let us, without a stoop, pick up our pearls
from shell and sand remembered,
sifting, gleaning
with the finest net of all
while waters wind through our castle
and our kingdom sinks to the sea.

Should we stand or sit?
(mattress is awash and bumping at the door)
use honeydarlingdears or only glances?
(names that melted once in sugartalk
now seem hardcold as our wet shoes)
say goodbye touching hands or at the lips?

Looking at us now
bent over bones of who we were,
oh, who would know
the beauty that has been?

LOVE'S A CRAZY SCRAPBOOK

Love's a crazy scrapbook:
necktie dangling on the chair,
my wristwatch just beyond our reach
winding phosphorescent moments
off the table edge that gleamed
the time of night we didn't care
we didn't care...

crazy scrapbook—
sock and stocking on the rug
some smiling Arabs sold me in the rain,
one black with hole beginning at the toe,
one beige with runs meandering to the thigh,
their careless mates both lying on the desk
where notepad reading "roses: don't forget"
held down the smallest finger of your glove...

pages flutter on my mind:
picture postcards of our days
of drift and sail,
of cliffside wine
and barefoot climb of grass to storied walls
high above some fall to guess and not believe,
and not believe...
but pages dim and scatter, album all
is grey to touch and chill to see
with sequence of our joys now shaken still,
slowstopped, reversed, like hourglass sand
dripped back to cancel, cover up
those promises to soulsave glitterings
from dust of roads remembered,
promises to keep cathedrals high,
each precipice approachable as silence in our glances,
our book mysterious in its plainest page.

But love's a crazy scrapbook:
our sand is rising blowing time

and tumbling pictures off the chain
our album was, while we go bound
in thinnest paper of it all,
reading our legend on ourselves,
stamped on us glittering,
high, in code approachable to memory
of episode as large as tale,
of crumbs much more than loaf,
of tatters warmer than a coat,
of rinds and peelings lush as orange
whole and bursting on the tree . . .

crazy scrapbook—
somewhere near the end
the pages will not hold; they mix
like shuffle at the bottom of a deck
some Majikmaker with a cynic flair
made easy till we tried
and almost made it
almost made it . . .

scrapbook: scraps
of what was love
were love at last
when finger on my neck was only little knot of tie
and pulsing at my hand
was only clock that ticked through all those nights
I didn't care, I said
I didn't care
though somewhere gloves and pantyhose
might spread as clear as glass
you must be holding now
to smooth your face of every sign
we made our own.

Oh, love's a crazy scrapbook
when it's closed.

TOPLESS, BOTTOMLESS BAR, MANHATTAN

Felt naked going in,
so fresh those lively bottoms
tossing at the door, crisscrossing drinks
with flavored arms that later pulled me down
with "Want me to sit with you?"
Breath needed for reply was sucked away
by tittywhirlings touchable right where my gaze
was teased by saxophone unseen,
their sudden sexy flesh a music-making
inviting secret words
I felt updrifting from my skin

aroused by Pretty Pickpocket—that gleaming girl up there
with gliding arms and tipping breasts:
without one pause, one glance at me,
she slid her fingers down my waist
and found my lyric for the song
those bobbing fellows leaning at her feet
drummed elbows to.

Along their beardless chins that ringed her upraised floor,
she bottomed slow on hips downsettling like a spinning coin
and squatted squarely in the face of one
who gawked at what she closely opened to his eyes,
himself a nested baby bird
long-necked with stretching, vulnerable and raw,
athrob to join-explore some warmly moving thing
needful as flesh upon his bone.

Transfixed in orange light that lovelied all her face,
that silenced in his ribs his fellows' poking jibes,
he tensed to manly posture she had powered in her thighs,
some sharp remembrance that took them both by red surprise
that louder saxophone and her snakier dance,
a turbulence revived and braying,
shook from the heaving air —
adrift the tiny babbling space he emptied with a laugh.

We men knew what to do: we grinned
behind our puff of insight,
hidden still.

ASS ON THE BEACH, IN SPAIN

So much of it was there,
golden, chocolate, and beige,
creamy tan and curvy brown,
my narrow bed tonight turns to remember
all the armfuls Spanish afternoons
took from the sea
and poured upon the sands of me.

Ass on the beach in Spain
dazzled my thighs,
sprayed fire upon the distances
that closed and opened
when it brushed me with its laces,
stringthing that played its touch of salt
across my chest in passing.
Oh, the heft of it
burned my trunks
with its changing flare.

Ass on the beach in Spain,
slimthing that spread to me
its patch of gayeties,
flowed me with warmweights to my toes,
pulled me to waters,
drained me of shores to hold,
anchored me to notions drifting to sea.

Ass on the beach,
I feel you,
always will.
Oh, rub your dare-you's on my thigh,
forest me with sapling gold
dewing my touch.
I reach across this night
to chocolate, and cream, and brown,
calling you no other name
but ass on the beach,
wherever Spain.

THE SQUEEZING OF THE BRA

"Don't squeeze my bra so tight," she said.
I eased up, felt her voice away,
deep-eyed her backing flesh enough
to pad the clatterflow of thoughts
my hand played fresh with,
chastened as it mini-squeezed her bra
to hang it on the bathroom line.

My unaccustomed wringing done,
her "Thanks for helping" floated in
from knock of kitchen dishes,
poured rhythms into hoverings of lace above me,
herself those dryings pink and yellow, green and blue
alerted to withdraw, slide down into one stinging riddle
centerheaped should I disturb their Plastic Mistress—
grey-metalled creature on the wall that spun them out
lushlooped and fragile.

"It's ready!" caught me sneezing on fluffstuff detergent,
jerking Kleenex from dispenser lower on the wall—
the Plastic Queen who chose to startle-mix me,
withdrawing in her pink flower window-mouth
her perfect inside-bra-shaped portion
torn living from my hand, my instant need.

At table, unreadied listening distracted,
I eased my heavyhanded mind away,
squeezed off a wish my eyes could follow,
her moving touchables one target,
the next her lace below, intensely visible
through curvy spoon and yellow napkin.

Slow wondering which half my squeezing held,
which Empress-twin was warm and which was time
full clatterless, unpink, ungreen
except for deepdyes long fed me
and wrung from femininities awash, far off
and idea-dangling, I gulped,
all greedy, drowningly in doubts
as courteous as air.
"Beg pardon, I was dreaming"
was bathroom line I strung clothwhite as table.

"Save that for night" she fastened to it,
smiling touched my arm
right where my fragile hope was clinging
to her plastic Ladies,
implacable in spinning colors careful as a child
deep-silent with his picture-book
his flesh alone can close.

"EVEN STEVEN," FLAG FOR A LOVER'S FEUD

"Even Steven!" they used to shout,
brutal boys, appeased
when bloodspot shirt gave straight payback for jack-knifed shoe,
when slingshot rock flew swift reply
to wooden arrow in the back:
long-feathered days of warrior camps
impregnable to pudding-chested spies
who gigglebraided their pink wrath
brooding out of sight, slow-reddening for battle—
two sweltering sexes

till intermarried, warrior and spy
(old treehouse raids and duels in the corn
long lost as kiddiemitten moldered in the park)
he angerthrills to bugle cry and she to winding horn
when rocked in killerlust,
woundmakers blistergripped,
bloodflushing deadly mutters from their hearts,
digging for poison-pointed arrows,
spatwords huge for final stoning

till breathing slows to normal,
though pulsing "Even Steven" cannot melt the bitter valve
each throat would spit like feather
stuck in sweat of rage gone plump—
no password to the tingling
any warrior thumb would bruise-out,
any spy would flatten, double-menaced since the day
she brooding cracked the code that paired them:
    (the mudhaired one with rock in hand is He
    while She has blood upon her braids)
remembering she what rock, what stain
so coupled them, unappeasable,
white flags out of sight,
only wound on wound to bind them,
lesions molding warrior to spy.

THE TOULOUSE POEMS

Part II

The Ones Who Did It

back-of-the-hand slap into bushes of life,
curse for breakfast, threat for lunch,
and for evening meal
lash and chain and pistol ball
leerlaughing.

THE ONES WHO DID IT

They caught the Black giants
in jungle sleep,
stranglecoffled king and queen and baby prince,
dungeoned these my very own,
the best,
across the fatal seas
of suicide and baffling flux
and anguish flushed from memory,
threw them to their knees, taught them prayers
for god of the New World,
mumblings for whipmasters.

are you the ones who did it?

They caught Black princes
by their warbling throats
and said "Like hell you will!"
feeding hatred deep to Douglass, Wright, and Hughes,
feeding it sharp to Malcolm, feeding it hard:
whiphand beat Frederick once and raised a manly scar,
cursemouth lashed Richard up his own great hill,
pushed Langston's Blackness in his face
until he hugged it there,
spiked Malcolm's path with devildeeds
until his armor bristled with all brave reply.

are you the ones who did it?
are you the ones who did it?

And in this New World still
for us whose sleep was tossed when giants fell
hate received's a thing to grow on,
roll round in, seeing self all over,
boil in, turning deeper Black
in sizzling thoughts, rehearsing
that hate received's a bastard boy
born fist in his mouth

born spitting back
born puncher of faces
counterkiller
searcher of him who aimed at him
deadly arrow, hate-stare,
back-of-the-hand slap into bushes of life,
curse for breakfast, threat for lunch,
and for evening meal
lash and chain and pistol ball
leerlaughing.

are you the ones who did it?
are you the ones who did it?
ARE YOU THE ONES WHO DID IT?

Your hate received's a load to build on,
pile with lumber of my life, leftovers
jagged with poor fittings, second tries,
lopsided with your mean tricks in shabby underclothes.
lean sticks fallen to fire inside my wall
that smolders on some inmost bone
all fleshless ageless changeless
marrow of intent
to feed-you-whip-you-curse-you-push-you-spike-you BACK
and pile you centuries high
with this shitty load.

And did you, do you, will you say
you're not the ones who did it?
not the ones who did it?
THE ONES WHO DID IT?

KICKASS

Kickass—bitch or bull—
takes world for stomping ground,
makemuscles in whatever gentle face
is smile, whatever trusting back
is bare to whiplash,
bent for load.

I, who live to say this,
saw him start.

Twice upon a time
there lived an ugly prince
whose ugly father,
the King of Kickass,
gave him magic powers
of travel and disguise.

I, who live to say this,
saw them grow.

Saw him white and straight
slopwiper in a Dublin bar,
jacketed and braided in his might,
give kickass to a blue-eyed boy
so hard he skidded through the door,
newspapers gutterslapping with the blow
but gathered to his arm anew
and brought back guiltless, sold
with smile Prince Kickass could not bruise.

I, who live to say this,
saw him next a woman,
travelling hard.

Saw her in Kansas City,
poor but motherdimpled,
aproned for a tiring chore,
spooning to slobbermouth that cooed
while with her stranger hand
she branded "kickass" hot
upon a jealous older cheek
that balked at milky spinach, babysauce of apple.
It was her month as Ugly Princess,
mommylove quicksplit like aging treetrunk
axed and whitened falling,
worrywounded to the core.

I, who live to say this,
saw him next a rich man,
far-travelled.

Saw him jungletoothed in Africa
fevered with the beat of longlimbs
Black and gliding on the grass
until his gunwhip plan to snatch and chain them
sprang itself to trap, to coffle gang, to barracoon,
to ship that bled and coughed across the seas
and came to nightmare rest
on shore where Kickass was the king
who hated Black that jeweled his crown
and fanned his path
and washed his feet
and robed his bones
and poured his wine
and pitypillowed his white hairs
till night he loudly died
with "Kickass! Kickass!" burning in his eyes
and wiring down his lips
to teach another bedside prince
his golden rule.

I saw it happen.

Saw the new king grab it up,
take it for sinew, nerve
and bone resolve,
for legacy to sit atop the hill
and Kickass-be and Kickass-think and Kickass-do
till Earthball, nearly done to death,
might sink for his toestool.

And I, who live to say this,
say this:
it came—oh, came!—to nightmare
for this Ugly Prince,
though twice upon a time
he was a King.

AFTER THE POETRY READING, BLACK

His friend, the red hair and tight jeans,
took back her pen, left me THIS piece of cake:
"He's disappointed"—meant this dude half down the aisle,
himself so blond surveying,
counting those who cared—
added what she meant, sweeping off the crumbs
with "You're not Black enough, he said."

But do they EVER say, I thought,
just what they mean?—and didn't even see
her fine retreat,
but went behind The Veil . . .

Back there with Truth, and Prosser, Turner,
whipped out my pocket Trans-a-lator
model Double-Oh-Daddy-o-Douglass,
pushed chromobuttons "Blond" and "Reddish,"
laid it 'longside the echoes in the aisle
till cake came back in Trans-a-lator slices
hard and sure as this:

"He's disappointed:
    wanted to frolic in the backyard of your mind,
    smell weeds, rip up the tender shoots, peel back the shade,
    white-backlash with his boots the darkest flowers.
"He's disappointed:
    wanted to squat on your kitchen floor,
    suck possum bones, juggle a hoecake,
    name thirteen kinds of greens You People know.
"He's disappointed:
    wanted to wave his shelf of Negro Books
    full in your face, back you up against the wall
    with itty-bitty black facts from White Muricana."
"You're not Black enough:
    not frothing at the mouth
    with whatchu-done-to-me's,
    not the Black Knight on the white horse
    weaned and gelded on Ole Massa's farm,
    not the Deppity Shuriff of Chitlin County,

first of the race tgit 'lected,
not the Fastest Popgun in the West,
not the President of the Bignig Club,
not even top contributor to TNT
(Truculent Negroes of the Town)."

Shook my Trans-a-lator, turned it upside down,
got this:

"What he REALLY means—
are you still listening?—
is this:
   wants to stick his foot in the trap—
   did you say 'WHAT trap?'—
   and pull it out safe, betterbooted,
   brand new with kickass sole and rubberclubber heel;·
   wants to drop dead from grief
   they forcefed down your daddy's throat,
   wants to choke and drown in the bloody wake
   where scores of you
     oh, once upon a time in chains
   together flung yourselves into the sea,
   wants style to fight the wolves and feed the lash
   and taste the worms and eat the trash,
   and Charlie-Hero of it all
   die upfront, gasping on the stage,
   yeah, wants you, the Deppity Shuriff, Black Knight,
   President with the white popgun,
   to shoot him down dead . . .
   while to applause, behind adoring screams,
   he crawls to life again,
   stands up The Man,
   junglemaker who in the dark
   created all—the trap, the chains, the wolves,
   himself as playmaker, adtaker,
   hawker of tickets to the show,
   auctioneer of stars
     oh, stars that once upon a time
     fell from the sky in chains of fire . . ."

Shirtpocketed my Trans-a-lator,
turned to leave the stage,
but stage itself seemed turning,
follow-moving, circling me,
enfolding me upfront—though I felt leaving down the aisle
not looking back—until some curtain rose
and audience was new, was Black,
was waiting.

Must be some trick my Trans-a-lator knew:
pushed in that chromobutton "Black"
and only heard the beating of my heart;
kept pushing it till floor rose up on sounds
like hoofbeats on the grass,
booBOOF-booBOOF-booBOOF, and faster,
till breath around was tight as if the climax of some play was on
and I was sitting in the crowd—
booBOOF-booBOOF-booBOOF was all the air—
the brother next to me turned like a page
close to my eyes;
"ThaCHU he talkin bout?" he said.
He meant the short Black man upfront
who meant the poem I mean to write
as I said "Yes"
up-coming from The Veil...

A neat, pale hand extended blocked my path
till I politely shook it, groping elsewhere in my mind
through new poems Black enough
(the shock that twitched his face said so)
to leave a scar.

"He's disappointed," I thought.

And I knew
what I meant.

A HARLEM ROMANCE

My friend betrayed me.
Armless grey
the only color worth today:
she broke windows of my needs,
crumbled stairways to all deeds
we swore to; now I swear
no future friend will walk my yard;
I will be hard,
be cold as summer snow,
be twice the peak
no one can climb.

My friend betrayed me.
I'll taste new clouds,
empty the cup we vowed to fill,
perch my pale husk of self
on leaf along the timber line
and build into the branchless air
a hut that has no step, no stair,
no single reaching thing
of fall,
no window looking out or in.

As I stood long to beg
this crust of pity,
a short black dog pissed on my leg.
Revived, I smelled my Harlem street
of magic stains,
its muscled colors bubbling in the sun,
behind The Veil its broken cups
usable as rain,
its splintered stairways peakable as trees,
windows never empty,
betrayals never wept.

Get a leg up otherwhere, I thought.
It's Harlem,
where streets keep walking.

THE WARSAW EXPERIMENT

Where was your crash helmet
when the darkest of them all—
the days, the words, the Warsaw wounds—
spilled you off the road,
you driving, playthinking for your life with both hands,
crying "Help me! Help me!"?

"THE WARSAW EXPERIMENT, '75-'76":
AN UNBORN PLAY

Promised you'd write it,
remember?
"The Warsaw Experiment" –
even the title would throb,
even for strangers would wake a feverish past,
would run painpulsing images that wilder run from running:
the surgeon's dagger, the pig-guard's bludgeonbadge,
statistics red with weeping, blurred with crossings-out.
X's marking all the spots that bleed.
But these were not the Warsaw that we knew,
these chains-and-barbed-wire notions
bloodtrue and legendary
as its forests of the dead.

Who would believe it?
The other ones who knew, who lived the year, are gone:
Nadine, who hunched cold in her corner and would not cry:
Jo Ann, so pretty that we all believed no one would harm her:
and Evelyn, whose loneliness grew claws that would not hide—
all only metaphors for you,
alive to stage their story,
the stagger in our nightwalk back
to that city of flowers,
where bouquets-of-three
could not live.

Some always will survive:
a little flowerfact in need of holding up,
in need of you,
who promised to pour it all out in a play,
swore it with both hands on your lips
while those greybrow winter days
stuck like dull teeth of an old comb
dropping out in your hair
listlessly
as you made faces in the mirror,
cross when each afternoon darkness at three
wrote "This day is cancelled."

The curtain did not rise:
although routine could not unteach your truths
that often made each Polish glance a stone to face,
each word a No, each touch a slab of closing door,
your every step a hunger-guess, obscurely punishable—
yet, each perch of rest you found
found you bereft of language strange enough
to give those daily dyings bone and stride,
the downdeep sag a shape, the cindered hopes a voice
to walk on stage, announcing "We are the Warsaw Experiment.
September to June."

What did you say to the actors,
who had nothing to say,
no audience to mourn?
Silence says they went away,
like Evelyn, Jo Ann, Nadine,
and the moneyback guarantee you pasted on your heart
came loose,
a fluttering, a flake-off of our hope
you'd really write it,
write for your life,
for the fever that ran in your arms
crying "Help me! Help me!"
when the dark afternoons didn't care.

Thought you'd write it with both hands
those days when words were spilling in your eyes
like stutterings,
those nights when scars that raised us from our beds
bled back to wounds,
to words so foreign to your lips
you swore some prompter must have said them:
some icebound Devil of the Vistula
practicing beneath the hoary bridge
playwriting straightest access to your heart
through Warsaw streets unknowable as woe—
    meanwhile the other strangeness warm to bear:

the costume-talk of diplomatic lips
feeding kindness to your ears,
American, Australian, British, Dutch,
above imported mushrooms buffet-style,
above each décolletage that swelled,
each veteran cravat that paced its fragrant rounds—
an international woe at play, those pretty people,
near guarantee against a fall.

Promised you'd never fall,
remember?
Where was your crash helmet
when the darkest of them all—
the days, the words, the Warsaw wounds—
spilled you off the road,
you driving, playthinking for your life with both hands,
crying "Help me! Help me!"?

That was a question.
This is a gift blown after you,
a flower to hold you up,
a kiss to catch you driving,
wheeling with both hands,
bloodnaming the memory
"The Warsaw Experiment."

A TALE OF POLISH HAM

Twice upon a time
I was a limping Pole;
came back unsteady with my medals, came back
with all my Polishness bent hungergleaming
on a tin of ham my eyes espied
low on a shelf three Pewex clerks hotel-wise
guarded with their Polish selves.

Connecting with them with my furtive nod
and bodytwist all focused on my country's ham,
I flourished what I knew was coin,
added to it superpowers of needy glance—
but all collapsed before the smiling fact
perfumed upon me in a Polish phrase
that mine were merely *zlotys*,
was merely dollar-hunger of the Warsaw kind,
was merely claim of blood
on miles of history.

My feet that used to ache,
my wounds that used to fire me in the night,
remembered.

Outside on the street, my Polishness restored,
I shook a Kruczka door that opened three stores in a row
and took my ham for granted—
my *zlotys* just as firm in hand
as polished rifle twice upon a time I held
saluting the straight general with the haggard face—

    but I did not find it,
    did not find it;
    they sent it out of the country—
    whoever THEY are—
    and it will not come back as proud as I—
    WHOEVER I am.

WOMEN OF WARSAW

Went shopping with you,
slipped invisible into your brooding circle,
enfolded silent as the empty baskets of your hearts
squeezed like the row of speckled fists
you clenched around the narrow throat of bin
where lumps of Rutkowskiego meat
were in a tightened moment package-poured,
a moment stupefying with all beatings
in my ear, your knocks and stomps
that shook my body with surprise

till something in me moved
like sliding rock pushed upward in its fall,
some looming snatch pried loose
from time and sense,
to jerk your lumps away,
swift from your very arms—
those brutal, tender arms—
with one reproach, this given me to say:
    "Only meat I see,
    pennypackages
    for all you were and are,
    flatpatties for the souls of you,
    lumpnotes for your songs."

And now it will not move,
this something in me
brooding
seeing faith you summon every day for strength,
for elbow craft and shoulder lore,
for poise of face beneath your granite mask
rehearsing every day its "I don't care"
while you must whip each bone into the crowds
to do its job: to live,
to clothe itself in meat,
and wait to sing its song.

POLITICAL POEM, FOR MONIKA OF WARSAW

You tried.

So this is for you, Monika,
heart of this sinking hole
my thoughtful toe is curving in the sand,
for all of us, digging this question:
    Why did you do it?

You tried,
shook the box hard,
wouldn't take No for an answer,
kept on shaking even when it smelled
and flipped up its badge, flashlit its blankface photo,
turned all its label ass-up, so you could see
who's sitting on you—
on all of us—
and read the price to pay.

You were a foolish girl:
the tears that hid behind your blinking eyes
were plain as bread in a peasant's basket
when you couldn't say you couldn't do it,
couldn't dump the box, couldn't cut the string,
couldn't stand the stench, couldn't even tear your hair
to music we might feel,
or walk away to rhythms deep enough to some day
dance your name back saying
    "She was our Warsaw friend."

But you tried,
and this for us was lift and stir,
was breath for what remained
to sleep on bruises,
to wither in corners of the bone
too tired to tremble.

This is for you,
who quit at last,
who left us standing in the dark
holding hands and tickets home,
with "Anything-you-say-will-do"
the answer
to the box that smelled.

Can you hear me?
Are you still there?
We speak of you—
    we two who couldn't take the shit,
    who couldn't take No for the answer—
think of you standing in the dark,
dream of you shaking the box again,
for all of us,
knifing the string, spilling the badge,
dumping ALL those faces ass-up.

You shake it,
Monika,
till the price is paid.

OCCASIONALS

So much begins in pain:

    a truth to raise my eyes,
    find you there waiting,
    your arms to catch, to hold,
    unrecognizable as saints,
    believable as wood within a stair

THE TWO-HOUR WAIT:
A READING FOR WIEN INTERNATIONAL

Taxi was a sagged balloon;
rainstreets to your patient door
were waverings, my ropelines to twist on,
shredding ifs and whethers, maybe-nots
on waters to cross unseeing,
unrecognizing even redlight pausings,
even the final stop
incredible as those goodbyes from people leaving
furry-clothed in had-to-go's and sorry's,
shudder of door behind them,
my passage through—
a tightness pulling close
those waiting faces.

Felt indecent sitting down,
corrupt receiving praises
(bent microphone dark witness of it all)
while sifting poems to best ignore
to paste across the two hours of your lives
gone empty—
hefting the unpayable debt,
suddenly thinking rhyme for you:
　　("Can this be all?
　　　Will you catch me / if I fall?")

So much begins in pain:

　　a truth to raise my eyes,
　　find you there waiting,
　　your arms to catch, to hold,
　　unrecognizable as saints,
　　believable as wood within a stair,
　　climbable to passage through
　　to loosenings, to air.

Now past, those streets of rain
to run to reach you
disappear,
but reachings, heftings of the doubt,
the waiting truth,
remain the rhyme,
believable as air.

VIENNA, HER FULBRIGHT BOOK

(*For Martha*)

"Go, litel bok."

With kiss upon the wind,
soulvapor, afterbreath,
a glistening from deepland heart
    of England
came Chaucer's lingering.

Six centuries too short a time
to fade the dedicating page
that tells the forelove, fumblings—
    hesitations all—
that wake and stir a book;

a poem too short a way to go
to see the moment
this Vienna vowed her book alive
with brimtouch firmed in wine
and midnight afterstroll
    in spiritsteps
of other travelers, servers of this space
their words would shine
and hush with Chaucer-wish:
"Go, little book,
    go."

(Dedicatory poem in *Interculture: a Collection of Essays and Creative Writing Commemorating the Twentieth Anniversary of the Fulbright Program at the Institute of Translation and Interpretation, University of Vienna (1955-1974),* ed. Sy M. Kahn and Mårtha Raetz [Vienna: Braumüller, 1975].)

UNWANTED PREGNANCIES:
CASELOAD ON THE JOB

(For Gwennie)

Toast sticks breakfast
down my throat,
stopping,
painthinking, Why?

Woman,
grimface girl,
the slouch on your chair heavy
with beat of life you want
to kill,
your name your name?
Case Number 7 today, you
were born? born where? where?

You behind her, you
with savage freckles,
with tender curl wethanging
on your cheek just from the rain,
downstaring as if floor were all you knew—
lover, friend, a fellowparent
awaiting turn to feel the pain—
while tiny fist is in my throat,
even before your turn I ask you hard
give me some corner of the truth
you spoon into the floor
with all your toe, and wipe so solemn.

You next one,
will you lie to me?
you with Blackness on your face
and other black spread on your mind
and Blackman laughing on your arm, a memory,
careless with his lies
that lovely touched your lips
and downcaressed your arms.
What musing in your hand
pulls at your dress, unwrinkling
smoothest place of all,
turning to rest at last where he
thought least to stay?

And you whose heels are high
and noisy till they stop beneath the seat
you sudden take,
you who will gumchew-lie to me
as easy as you toss your hair,
who need no solace in light of day,
swinger of the cup that never fills,
how goes it with you
as toast at last goes down?

Coffeesip is all I get
to stand me up to face the day,
same as for you now facing me,
a   new one,
barely standing there and
(sit-down-save-your-strength)
pronouncing
your name.

KITCHEN GIRL: A LOVE POEM

Spicetime ticking.
Even dulldays care.
Kitchen windows needing air,
like packages of basil, poppy seeds and dill,
like lovers in their moody times—
most of all, sweet seasonings
sealed, thinpapered fine—
ought open   slow.

But paper torn too quick and deep,
at edges wrong, spills
oh! the stream-surprise
    when the marvelous curry uncaught
    disappears down the drain,
    when the angry Paprika
    throws his redpepper kiss
    back through stains on the air,
    when the laurel drops crushed
    in the bay leaves her grasp tries to hold,
    when sweet Marjoram, feeling his wildness,
    remembering purples and pinks,
    takes the tear in his cap for excuse
    for goodbye.

Lift of cap can hurt,
can unjar spice and spill the sweet—
wrongtimed but set to fit the wrench
some wayward day will pause
to twist into each momentary art:
    then cinnamon cascade will fall,
    like ginger-sugar-clove
    alive in shookoff air at shoulder-height
    soon lingerbreath as spiceless as an empty cap
    dryfitting none.

Spicethings run down,
run away,
sting of beauty all their art,
in or out of every heart.

ABOUT THE AUTHOR

A Nebraskan through high school, James A. Emanuel lived in Colorado, Kansas, Iowa, Illinois, and Washington, D.C., before settling in New York, where he earned his Ph.D. from Columbia in 1962. He teaches at the City College of New York, where he introduced the study of Black poetry in 1966. He has taught Black literature in France and Poland, and has read widely from his works in Europe, Africa, and America. Among his many publications, he values especially the pioneering **Langston Hughes** (1967) and **Dark Symphony: Negro Literature in America** (1968), his poetry volumes, and the five Broadside Critics Series books that he edited—the first such Black series in America.